Life in Ponds and Streams

A painted turtle suns itself near a white water lily.

by William H. Amos

BOOKS FOR YOUNG EXPLORERS
NATIONAL GEOGRAPHIC SOCIETY

COPYRIGHT © 1981 NATIONAL GEOGRAPHIC SOCIETY   LIBRARY OF CONGRESS CIP DATA: P. 32

On a warm spring day, a boy named Michael walks with his father beside a quiet stream. They are going to a pond deep in the woods. There is hidden life all around them. What will they find?

Michael hears rustling in the bushes and splashing in the stream.
Ripples move across the surface of the water.
Michael wonders what animals live in the water and nearby.

BEAVER LODGE

Beavers live in ponds and streams.
These beavers are inside
their lodge, a house built of sticks.
Michael discovers a tree that
beavers have chopped down
with their sharp teeth. Beavers
eat parts of trees, water lilies,
and some other plants.

4

BEAVER PULLING A WATER LILY

Michael stands at the edge
of the pond and looks around.
He sees a large dragonfly
resting on a plant.
A water snake glides
across a water lily.
"Stay very still and let
the animals come near you,"
says Michael's father.
There are many surprises
waiting for the two of them.
What will happen next?

TEN-SPOT DRAGONFLY

BANDED WATER SNAKE

Baby painted turtles are hatching from their eggs
that have been discovered near the pond. Each turtle
is about the size of a quarter. The turtles can swim as soon
as they hatch. They will scramble down to the safety of the pond.
Painted turtles are good swimmers. They hunt for food underwater.
A full-grown turtle warms itself on a log in the morning sun.

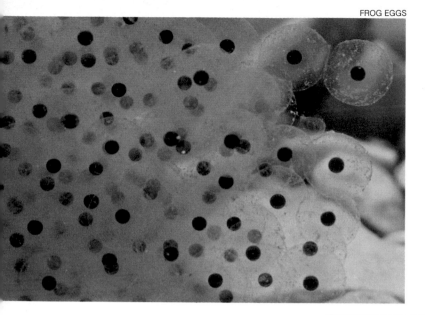

Up jumps a frog
on its long back legs!
The frog will strike
at any small animals
moving by. Insects are
its main food. The dragonfly
on the water lily is not too big
for the hungry frog to eat.

Frog eggs look like
small beads of jelly.
Each egg soon hatches
into a fishlike tadpole.
Michael has scooped
some tadpoles
from the shallow water
at the edge of the pond.
They feed there
on tiny plants
called algae.
Later, they grow legs.
Their tails disappear.
They spend more and
more time on land.
What does a tadpole
become? A small frog!

TADPOLES

10

A big green frog floats in the water, where many insects live.
The frog catches insects with its long, sticky tongue.
The whirligig beetle with its bubble of air can escape underwater.
But the water strider will be gobbled up if it comes too close.
The back swimmer rises to the surface of the water to breathe,
and it may be caught there by the watching frog.

WHIRLIGIG BEETLE

WATER STRIDER

BACK SWIMMER

The surface of the water is
a floor for the water strider.
For the whirligig beetle,
the surface is also a ceiling.
It is often a ceiling
for the back swimmer, too.

Splash! A male mallard duck springs up from the water.
The female mallard and her five ducklings swim quietly
along the shore, where they may disappear among the plants.
Ducklings always follow close behind their mother.
Why are they hard to see when they are near the shore?
Their brown feathers blend in with the plants growing there.

RED EFT

Michael and his father
leave the pond and
walk back to the stream.
On the way, Michael sees
a brightly colored eft
crawling on the bank.
"An eft is the young of
one kind of salamander,"
explains Michael's father.
Soon it will become
a green-and-brown adult.
Then it is called a newt.
Newts live underwater.

A pair of otters watches
from a rock beside a stream.
Their webbed feet help them
swim well. One otter glides
through the clear water.
A furry raccoon hunts
for crayfish to eat.
The raccoon is a visitor
from the nearby woods.

Michael has found
an opening to
the burrow where
a crayfish lives.
Balls of mud
form a chimney
above the hole.

A crayfish has two large claws.
It uses the claws to grab food
and to defend itself.
An otter has cornered a crayfish.
By raising its claws,
the crayfish may surprise
the otter and be able to escape.

What a strange-looking creature this is! It is the larva of a caddis fly.
It will change into an adult insect. The larva lives underwater.
It builds a case out of sticks or tiny pebbles. The case
may protect it from hungry fishes and from the fast-moving water.

NET-BUILDING CADDIS FLY LARVA

Michael feels how swiftly the water flows along.
At the bottom of the stream, another kind of caddis fly larva
has made a fishing net of silky thread. The net catches
small animals and plants from the water. Then the larva comes
to eat the food it has caught. The larva will change into a pupa.
The pupa will become an insect with wings.

ADULT CADDIS FLY

23

Many animals live on rocks
at the bottom of the stream.
The water is quieter there.
What will Michael and
his father find on this rock?
They may see the young
of different insects.

FISH FLY LARVA

STONE FLY NYMPH

A fish fly larva hunts for food underwater. And so does
another young insect, called a stone fly nymph.
A round, flat water penny can cling to rocks. The water flows over it.

WATER PENNY, LARVA OF A RIFFLE BEETLE

Creek chub swim together in a shallow stream.
These silvery fish eat insects and bits of plants.
Sometimes they eat smaller fishes, too. A spotted snail
crawls over moss on the bottom of the stream.
The snail feeds there on algae and other water plants.

The beautiful brook trout can swim
through very swift water.
The sculpin lives on the bottom,
where the water is quieter.
A full-grown brook trout may catch
a slimy sculpin for food.

BROOK TROUT

SNAIL

SCULPIN

A green heron has just caught
a minnow in its long bill.
The heron waits in shallow water
for food. Because the bird
stays so still, it is hard to see.
It darts forward in an instant
to make its catch.
Once it spots a fish or a frog,
it almost never misses.

These baby green herons have
hatched in their nest. The nest
is in a tree above the water
where their parents fish.

Michael finds a deer track
in soft ground beside the stream.
Deer visit streams and ponds
at night and in the early morning
to drink the cool water.
If Michael waits until dusk,
he may see a deer.
He has already seen
many other kinds of animals.

Michael and his father have watched
some animals that live in streams
and some that live in ponds.
They have made many discoveries,
and they have had some surprises, too.
Michael will never forget this day.

Published by The National Geographic Society
Gilbert M. Grosvenor, *President;* Melvin M. Payne, *Chairman of the Board;*
Owen R. Anderson, *Executive Vice President;* Robert L. Breeden, *Vice President,
Publications and Educational Media*

Prepared by The Special Publications Division
Donald J. Crump, *Director*
Philip B. Silcott, *Associate Director*
William L. Allen, William R. Gray, *Assistant Directors*

Staff for this Book
Margery G. Dunn, *Managing Editor*
Alison Wilbur, *Picture Editor*
Marianne R. Koszorus, *Art Director*
Stephen Hubbard, *Researcher*
Carol A. Rocheleau, *Illustrations Secretary*

Engraving, Printing, and Product Manufacture
Robert W. Messer, *Manager*
George V. White, *Production Manager*
David V. Showers, *Production Project Manager*
Mark R. Dunlevy, Richard A. McClure, Raja D. Murshed, Christine A. Roberts, Gregory Storer, *Assistant Production Managers*
Mary A. Bennett, Katherine H. Donohue, *Production Staff Assistants*

Debra A. Antonini, Nancy F. Berry, Pamela A. Black, Nettie Burke, Jane H. Buxton, Claire M. Doig, Rosamund Garner, Victoria D.
    Garrett, Virginia A. McCoy, Cleo Petroff, Victoria I. Piscopo, Tammy Presley, Katheryn M. Slocum, Jenny Takacs, *Staff Assistants*

Consultants
Dr. Glenn O. Blough, Peter L. Munroe, *Educational Consultants*
Lynda Ehrlich, *Reading Consultant*
Staff, Smithsonian Institution; Dr. Laurence Tilly, Center for Environment and Energy Research, University of Puerto Rico, *Scientific
    Consultants*

Illustrations Credits
Zig Leszczynski, ANIMALS ANIMALS (cover, 1, 8-9); National Geographic Photographer Joseph H. Bailey (2-3, 5 right, 6, 10 lower, 17 upper, 20,
23 upper right, 24 upper, 30 left, 30-31 lower, 32 lower left); Jen and Des Bartlett (4-5, 19); William H. Amos (4 lower, 12-13 all except 13 center, 16-17,
23 upper left, 24-25 all except 24 upper left, 26-27 lower, 27 lower right); Gary Randall, TOM STACK & ASSOCIATES (5 lower); Edmund Appel, National
Audubon Society Collection, Photo Researchers (7 upper); J. H. Robinson, ANIMALS ANIMALS (7 lower); Jan L. Wassink, TOM STACK & ASSOCIATES
(9 upper); G. I. Bernard, Oxford Scientific Films (10 upper); National Geographic Photographer Bianca Lavies (11, 13 center); Tom Walker, TOM STACK
& ASSOCIATES (14-15); Charles Palek, ANIMALS ANIMALS (15 upper); © Jeff Foott, BRUCE COLEMAN INC. (18 upper); Stouffer Enterprises, Inc.,
ANIMALS ANIMALS (18 lower, 20-21); Breck P. Kent, ANIMALS ANIMALS (21 upper, 27 upper right); © Hans Pfletschinger, Peter Arnold, Inc. (22-23);
G. I. Bernard, ANIMALS ANIMALS (23 lower); E. R. Degginger (26-27 upper); Karl Maslowski (28-29); Lynn M. Stone, ANIMALS ANIMALS (29);
Leonard Lee Rue III, ANIMALS ANIMALS (30-31 upper); Dick Van Halsema, Jr. (32 lower right).

Library of Congress CIP **Data**
Amos, William Hopkins.
    Life in ponds and streams.

    (Books for young explorers)
    Summary: An introduction to the animals that live in ponds and streams, including beavers, frogs, ducks, crayfish, trout, and insects.
    1. Pond ecology—Juvenile literature. 2. Stream ecology—Juvenile literature. [1. Pond animals. 2. Stream animals] I. National Geographic Society (U. S.) II. Title. III. Series.
QH541.5.P63A48   591.5'26322   81-47745
ISBN 0-87044-404-2 (regular binding)   AACR2
ISBN 0-87044-409-2 (library binding)

Michael walks carefully across a log over the stream. He looks for small animals among the water lilies at the pond's edge.

Cover: A green frog rests on a log in water covered with duckweed.